A Heart's Journey Through Poetry

by

Shannan Lee Williams

A Heart's Journey Through Poetry

By

Shannan Lee Williams

DEDICATION

THIS BOOK IS DEDICATED TO MY CHILDREN, WHO ARE MY REASON FOR GETTING UP EACH DAY.

I WANT TO SAY THANK YOU TO MY MOTHER FOR BEING THERE AT A MOMENT'S NOTICE (AT ALL HOURS) THROUGHOUT WRITING THESE POEMS; LISTENING TO ME RE-WORD THEM OVER AND OVER AGAIN.

I ALSO WANT TO THANK MY GRANDMOTHER FOR HER PATIENCE WITH ME THROUGH THIS WHOLE ORDEAL.

I NEED TO THANK MY BEST FRIEND BELINDA FOR BEING THERE LISTENING TO ME READ EACH AND EVERY POEM TO HER, WHETHER SHE WANTED TO HEAR IT OR NOT. WE LAUGHED AND CRIED THROUGH THEM, AS THE MEMORIES FLOWED.

LAST BUT NOT LEAST, THANK YOU TO MY EDITOR... ROBYN KIRKEY WALKER, WHO IS VERY TALENTED AND HELPED ME TURN THESE POEMS INTO AMAZING PIECES OF ART.

TABLE OF CONTENTS

Section 1
(Love and Romance)

TABLE OF CONTENTS

Section 2

(This And That)

TABLE OF CONTENTS

Section 3

(Friends, Family and Encouragement)

A Heart's Journey Through Poetry

BY

Shannan Lee Williams

SECTION 1

(LOVE AND ROMANCE)

BREATHE

~

Breathe

Coming closer

Breathe

It has been so long

Eye contact

Seeing each other

Walking faster

Suddenly he is right in front of me

I freeze

Arms come around

Holding tight

Tears of joy in both of our eyes

Kiss me

Lips on mine

Can't breathe

SHANNAN LEE WILLIAMS

COULD YOU BE THE ONE FOR ME

~

Gentle, patient and kind

Absolutely blowing my mind

The little things you do

Whenever I'm around you

Giving you my heart

Knew it from the start

You are the one for me

First Kiss

~

Gentle fingers touch my face

Leaning my cheek into your hand

Closing my eyes

Soft but firm lips against mine

Running your fingers through my hair

My hands around your neck

A moan escapes your lips

This is the end of our perfect first kiss

SHANNAN LEE WILLIAMS

Head Over Heels

~

Head over heels

Falling for you

My head is spinning

So into you

Making me blush

Things you say

I'm under your spell

Want to stay

I Love You

~

Planning our future together

Finally, a complete family

Never dreamed I would be accepted for just being

me

Coming through every time

Proving yourself over and over

Truly a gift from God

Blessed to have found the love of my life

I love you with all my heart

Don't ever forget

Never doubt

My love is here to stay

SHANNAN LEE WILLIAMS

I Need You

~

I need you

Want you

Have to have you

All my dreams

My fantasies

Have all come true

I found love

Have hope

Now I'm with you

MY HERO

~

Out of nowhere

Sweeping me off my feet

A real man

My prince charming

Still believe in fairytales

Now that you are here

Happier than ever

My one true fated love

SHANNAN LEE WILLIAMS

SEEING YOU

~

Palms are sweating

Knees are weak

Heart is racing

Stomach full of butterflies

Knowing I'm about to see you

Hard to breathe

Can't even eat

Nearly falling

Can't stop smiling

Now that I'm here seeing you

Thank You For Loving Me

~

It's not easy loving me

I let my problems take over at times

Through it all

You are always there

Without complaining

You keep on loving me

Through the ups and downs

The twists and curves

Through thick and thin

Thank you for loving me

SHANNAN LEE WILLIAMS

This Must Be Love

~

Sweaty palms

Stomach full of butterflies

Trying to speak

Nothing comes out

Coming closer

Start to blush

Only thing on my mind

Morning, noon and night

Start talking

Feeling comfortable

Free and alive

Spending more time together

So easy to see

This must be love

We Can Make It Through Anything

~

You say you will always love me

Will never hurt me

Always be by my side

My trust in you is complete

Never has my heart felt this much

Having God at the head of this relationship

As long as we keep him number one

Follow his lead

This love will make it through anything

SHANNAN LEE WILLIAMS

You Are My Rock

~

I love your strength

Love your confidence

Love how no matter what I say

You assure me

You say that we'll make it through anything

As long as we have each other

There is nothing you won't do for me

I believe that

You constantly strive to make me happy

Keeping my love for you alive

You are my rock

You are my everything

You're Mine

~

You're mine, I'm yours

You said you knew it all along

Secretly I held it in

Now I can't imagine my life without you

My every wish and dream came true

Never knew a man like you could even exist

You got me baby with that amazing kiss

My life, my love, to you I give

Never would've thought I could love someone the

way I do you

All my faith and trust is in you

Suddenly I have this chance at love

You are the keeper of my heart

Apparently you knew this would be from the start

Shannan Lee Williams

You were planning on stealing my heart with that
kiss

ALL I NEED

~

All I need is love

All I want

Desire

You

All I need is trust

All I treasure

Crave

You

All I need is hope

All I know

Passion

You

SHANNAN LEE WILLIAMS

DAYS, HOURS, AND MINUTES

~

Patience wearing thin

Excited to see you again

Hard being away from you

A love so real, deep, and true

Counting down the days

So many ways

Show my love for you

Just like when it was new

Counting down the hours

Going to devour

You and me

Meant to be

Counting down the minutes

Cannot even sit

Run to each other

Kisses, one after another

SHANNAN LEE WILLIAMS

Do You Remember That Night

~

Do you remember that night

Saw you walking towards me

The moonlight shone so bright

I felt so alive and free.

Do you remember that night

Danced on the street

Underneath the stop light

Our lips finally had the chance to meet.

Do you remember that night

It began to pour

Safe and warm I knew it was right

You held me and I desired you more.

Do you remember that night

Walked me home in the dark

Nothing had ever felt so right

That kiss surely ignited a spark.

How Intense

~

How intense
Feelings for you
Breathtaking
What I think of you.
How intense
Thoughts of you
Mesmerizing
When I think of you.
How intense
Dreams about you
Fantasizing
While I think of you.

I Am Loved

~

Tender words whispered in my ear

You know what I want to hear

Say I'm cute, wonderful and sweet

A man like you can't be beat

You would do anything for me you say

How about stay right here with me today

Would lay down your life for a woman like me

Guess this is how love is meant to be

Every wish and dream I've ever had has come

true

One look in your brown eyes and I feel anew

You're the best thing to ever happen to me

Want the whole world to see

I have been blessed from up above

I am loved

SHANNAN LEE WILLIAMS

Lotions And Potions

~

I've got you under my spell

Got you going through these motions

Feeling like you fell

I've got you with these lotions and potions.

I've got you glowing

Spinning and spinning

I've got you flowing

Now I'm the one who's winning.

Boy you're under my spell

Feels like an explosion

You mix well

With these lotions and potions.

You're starting to come undone

What a night we had

Looks like we both won

It sure beats being sad.

SHANNAN LEE WILLIAMS

LOVE AND UNDERSTANDING

~

Love and understanding is what you need

Always be here

No one else for me

Only you

Put your hand in mine

Trust in me

Giving you all of me

Want to show you how love is meant to be

No One Needs To Know

~

I've got this huge crush

Think of you I get a rush

I want to tell you so

No one needs to know

Chills run up and down my spine

When your face comes in my mind

I can't believe how much you turn me on

When I hear the words to a certain song

When you walk by me

I feel so giddy

Oh I want to tell you so

But no one needs to know

This is my fantasy

I'll keep this just for me

SHANNAN LEE WILLIAMS

We'll never know if we had something that could

grow

And I'll always wonder if you really needed to

know

Old Enough To Know Better

~

You're too old for me

They say I can do better

This is my life and I can make my own decisions

They say I'm old enough to know better

I say I'm old enough to know true love

I know a real man when I see one

Never felt love like this

True, genuine, and sincere

I see a strong trustworthy man

Who can safely hold my heart in the palm of his hand

They say I'm old enough to know better

I say I'm old enough to know that I love what I see

You are the kind of man that I read about in fairytales

SHANNAN LEE WILLIAMS

Prince charming, hero, knight in shining armor

You are all mine

I say I'm old enough to know better that I'm not

letting you go

To Love You

~

To love you is to need you

The way the flowers need the rain

To love you is to want you

So much it drives me insane

To love you is to feel you

Loving me back the same

To love you is to know you

You put all others to shame

To love you is to look at you

The way you look at me too

To love you is to touch you

I know our love is true

SHANNAN LEE WILLIAMS

You Are Home To Me

~

In your arms

The only place for me

Falling asleep, waking up

You are home to me

Next to you

Where I want to be

Forever you and I

You are home to me

The Letter

~

Listening intently

Squeaky brakes

Heartbeat quickens

My house is next

Anticipating

Mailbox opens

Something is set inside

Closes

Engine roars

Running to mailbox

Open

Reaches inside

Pulls out a letter

Looks at the address

Stops breathing

SHANNAN LEE WILLIAMS

Heart is racing

Runs to the house

Races upstairs

Slams bedroom door

Jumps on the bed

Holds letter close

Looks at the writing

Tears falling

Biting lip

Opening letter

Starting to read

Pure bliss

Loss and Heartache

~

I Won't Forget You

I'm someone I never knew

All my thanks goes to you

You seemed so perfect, too good to be true

I won't forget you

You taught me how to smile

That it's okay to cry once in a while

You told me to be strong; to begin anew

I won't forget you

You said you believed in me

That someday I would see

The words you told me were true

I won't forget you

Now when I look in the mirror

I don't see any more fear

SHANNAN LEE WILLIAMS

Everything you said was true

I won't forget you

Why did you have to leave

I still need you here with me

God has other plans for you

I won't forget you

That Hurts

~

Said you would always love me

Never would place anyone before me

You are with her now

Thought I was the best for you

No one ever did the things I did for you

Her hand you are holding now

Said I was your soul mate

We were brought together by fate

Her lips are the ones you are kissing now

I thought you would be forever true

I see we are forever through

She is the one you are walking away with now

That hurts

SHANNAN LEE WILLIAMS

FALLING OUT OF LOVE

~

Talked every night

Then every other night or so

Soon a text here and there

Now nothing.

Heart is breaking

Trying to figure out what went wrong

Won't return any of my calls

Tears falling.

Falling out of love

Is what is really happening

Must get used to it

Moving on.

SECTION 2
THIS AND THAT

SHANNAN LEE WILLIAMS

PANIC ATTACK

~

One arm goes numb

Feels like my jaw is going numb

The rest of my body on one side goes numb

Stabbing pains to chest

Take a pill

Wait for it to work

Slowly numbing goes away

Chest doesn't hurt anymore

Lie down and close my eyes

Back to sleep I go

A Wonderful Place

~

There's a place I like to go to get away from it all

To get away from like and its problems

And just relax for a while

To be by myself and not have to deal with

anything else

My mind is a wonderful place

SHANNAN LEE WILLIAMS

Night Time

~

Darkness begins to fill the night sky

The birds have all stopped chirping

All animals are scurrying to their homes

As the night prepare to fly

Springtime

~

The sun brings like to a new day

The bees start to sing their song

As they go from flower to flower

Collecting honey along the way

SUMMERTIME

~

The smell of saltwater in the air

Sand squishing between my toes

Cold water sends chills up my spine

Slippery seaweed wraps around my feet

Hot sun beats upon my back

Cold drink refreshes my mouth

Beach balls flying through the air

Ah the joys of summer

SHANNAN LEE WILLIAMS

SECTION 3

(FRIENDSHIP AND ENCOURAGEMENT)

IF I COULD

~

If I could take away your pain

Would take it for my very own

It kills me to see you like this

Wish you would let me help you

I can be there for you if you let me

Someone you can talk to and trust

If you would give me a chance

I could be a good friend

SHANNAN LEE WILLIAMS

IT MATTERS

~

You think you're all alone

Have nothing to live for

Three kids in the living room

It matters to them.

You say, "I give up, Lord, why me

I can't do this anymore

It's just too hard

I'm all alone"

It matters to Him.

You say, I'm doing the best I can

I'm only one person

I can only do so much"

It matters to me.

You tell me, "Thank you so much

I couldn't have done this without you

You are my best friend"

It matters to you.

Don't Wish It Away

~

One day they are two

The next they are thirty-two

Don't wish it away

Time goes too fast

Play with your kids

Love them, hug them, kiss them

Tell your kids you love them

One day they will be out on their own

Cherish these moments

They are yours to treasure

Can never be replaced

But will remain in your heart

FRIENDSHIP

~

There's something special about a friend

In whom you can confide in

Trust and share

Personal parts of your life

Without be criticized or judged

With whom you can be yourself

Laugh, cry, and just be silly

Be there cheering you on

A friend to be there when the rest of the world

has gone

SHANNAN LEE WILLIAMS

My Best Friend

~

There isn't anything you haven't done for me

Have always been there

Never met a friend like you

With whom I can be so completely myself

Never been able to be so honest

Or able to trust

We know each other's deepest darkest secrets

You would never leave me behind

Would walk through fire if it meant saving me

Always know what to say

Telling me the truth even if it's not what I want to hear

Making things right when I can't see any way out

The best kind of friend there is

One that I don't want to live without

Thank You For Being My Friend

~

Thank you for being my friend

Always there when I need you

Sticking up for me

Listening to me go on for hours

Even when it is about nothing at all

Thank you for your support

Catching me when I fall

Picking me back up

Being the greatest friend of all

SHANNAN LEE WILLIAMS

Shine On

~

You are such a special young lady

With a beautiful spirit

Always giving to others

Never expecting anything in return

You have a passion for the things that you love

A laugh that's contagious

An innocent smile

I love to watch you dance and listen to you sing

It's what makes you the happiest

The way your face lights up shows you're giving it

your best

You will succeed

Keep your sweet spirit

You will be amazing

You're already someone very special to me

YOU ARE BEAUTIFUL

~

You are beautiful

Inside and out

If someone tells you different

They are just jealous

Don't listen to those lies

You are a child of God

He makes no mistakes

God made you beautiful

Go out there and shine

Let the world see who you are

Dance and have fun

Shine, Shine, Shine

SHANNAN LEE WILLIAMS

I BELIEVE IN YOU

~

Anything is possible

Don't let anyone stand in your way

You're very smart

Have the power to succeed

Make a difference

Follow your heart

Your dreams

Put God number one

Following His lead

You won't go wrong

THANK YOU FOR READING. IF YOU ENJOYED THIS BOOK, PLEASE LEAVE YOUR REVIEW ON AMAZON.

ABOUT THIS AUTHOR

SHANNAN IS A SINGLE MOM WITH A PASSION FOR READING AND WRITING. SHE HAS ALWAYS WANTED TO BE A WRITER AND NOW HER DREAM HAS COME TRUE. SHE IS EXCITED TO SHARE HER HEART WITH THE READING WORLD.

HER WISH IS TO INSPIRE OTHERS TO PERSEVERE TO ACCOMPLISH THEIR DREAMS. SHE WANTS TO BLESS OTHERS THE WAY SHE HAS BEEN BLESSED.

Made in the USA
Middletown, DE
07 April 2018